Winter Texans
(Or)

The QTip Invasion
Of The Rio Grande Valley

2000 and 2001
Winter Texan Edition

Second Printing

Alan C. Tibbetts

Copyright © MIM
Alan C. Tibbetts

All rights reserved. This book, or parts thereof, may not be used or reproduced in any manner without written permission.

ISBN: 0-7392-0231-6

Printed in the USA by
Morris Publishing
3212 East Highway 30
Kearney, NE 68847

1-800 650 7888

Preface

As Kathy and I were driving north towards Corpus Christi, we noticed a lot of recreational vehicles with the drivers headed south. In unison we said, "They are back!" Right on schedule, Winter Texans were headed for the Rio Grande Valley.

I pondered such things as the destination of each driver, wondered if this was their first Valley experience, and if someone would tell them the ins and outs of the Valley.

On my first venture into this Valley I was not sure what I might find, or who I would get to know. After a few years of such seasonal stays I simply moved to the Valley.

I could have used some advice about what one can expect. This book, a "Winter Texan Survival Manual", will help you, especially if this is your first visit. With this in mind, I wrote this book.

Welcome to the Valley, and I hope this second edition will give you some insight as to what to expect. Go ahead, spend your money, meet new friends, forget the snow drifts and have a good time.

Remember, "You can't take it with you." Tell that to your wife who wants to bring her sewing machine, or your husband, his computer.

Alan C. Tibbetts

"Kathy, this is **not** the Rio Grande Valley!"

Contents

1. The Geriatric Maturation Process
   (Or)
   How Did We Get To This Age?...1
2. Adieu Nomenclature To A New One
   (Or)
   From "Snow Birds" to Winter Texans"......................6
3. Multifarious Species Propagate Trouble
   (Or)
   10% Cause 90% of The Problems.............................13
4. Insular/Indigenous Personnel Tethered
   (Or)
   Winter Texans and Locals Work Well Together...............16
5. Where Insular Earthlings Inhabit
   (Or)
   Some Communities Where Winter Texans Stay 27
6. Que Haciastuen Mexico?
   (Or)
   What Do You Do In Mexico?.......................................45
7. Cognitive Reference The RGV
   (Or)
   The Story of the Rio Grande Valley................................53
8. Our Portentous Linear Asylum
   (Or)
   Our Changing Family Structure..................................68
9. Dissection Parcel Replications
   (Or)
   Questions And Some Answers....................................78
10. Godspeed Legions Species
    (Or)
    Good-bye To Many Friendly People.............................86
    About The Author 90

ACKNOWLEDGEMENTS

Gene Washburn, internationally known artist, former Winter Texan, now a permanent resident on the Island, sketched the illustrations included in this book.

Veteran TV newsman, Johnny Goodman, host of the Winter Texan Report on Channel 4, cautiously but graciously introduced the book to his viewing audience. His twice daily report is a must for Winter Texans.

Allie Johnson, of the McAllen Monitor, developed a novel and most effective article for that newspaper. My mailbox was full of copies of the front page presentation, sent by well-wishers.

Johnny Rodriguez, of TV Channel 5, both filmed and narrated a well-watched news introduction to the book.

The Winter Texan attendees at the Chapel By The Sea, South Padre Island, and my place of worship, dared me to write such a book as this. Most of the contents of the book came from them.

Renee Skala and Wendy Peterson of Morris Publishers were always ready to assist me in the development of this little volume. The only suggestion I can make is that they might consider bringing their operation to the Rio Grande Valley.

MORE ACKNOWLEDGEMENTS

To the Winter Texans who read the book and called or wrote to tell me of their impressions. It is always good to have feedback when one tries to communicate ideas. The first printing was sold out in ninety days.

To the following establishments where readers could find the book:

Desert Bloom Bookstore, 2104 Griffin Pkwy, Mission. Texas, 78572

Book World. 400 Nolana, McAllen, Texas, 78504

Blue Marlin Supermarket, 2912 Padre Blvd, South Padre Island, Texas, 78597

Little Bit of Texas, 3812 Padre Blvd, South Padre Island, Texas 78597

T-Shirt Warehouse, 3800 Padre Blvd, South Padre Island, Texas 78597

Port Isabel Historical Museum, Port Isabel, Texas. The new museum is excellent, one you would do well to visit

This book is produced in larger print size for the mature reader.

(It also enables the author to read what he wrote)

Chapter One

The Geriatric Maturation Process
(Or)
How Did We Get To This Age?

Time has a subtle way of going by. It seems only yesterday we were children, looking forward to those days when we could be our own boss. Those were the longest days we lived. We could not be convinced that at some point in life we would be able to call the shots in life. Then that day came.

The rest of our lives seem to be a blurred memory of years passing by. I do not know if it is the same with you, but the older I get, the better I was.

Our early youth was spent in learning, yearning, and playing. We developed a number of friends and we became a part of a larger group of like people. We were really gang members, but not like it might sound. We went to the movies as a gang, and ate at drive-ins as a gang. We were individuals, but our daily behavior was determined by our friends, and in some cases, our terrified parents. We had to decide whether or not to listen to our gang or our parents. Usually we listened to our gang.

Then something began to happen. The gangs became smaller and we learned to run around in pairs, normally a boy with a girl. We were in love. We forgot that gang stuff.

"George," said his buddy, "do you think there is as much love as there used to be?" "You bet," said George, "there is just a different bunch doing it."

As young adults we began to forsake the old gang and cling to that one special person. Sometimes we did so much clinging that we found the results to be tiny babies.

Our hopes that we could do whatever we wished to do were dashed. Our parents were not telling us what to do but the neonates certainly knew how to change our well-made plans.

The era of rearing children began, and ended some eighteen years later. For all these years, our society changed. We did not have the time to get away from the "ankle biters", and we had less money to go around. As a result, we began to do more dining in the home, not because we wanted to, but simply because we had little money to pay for a nice meal, on top of paying a baby-sitter.

Our old pals were largely in the same boat. They were grounded by their children. Old friendships began to wane, or at least put on the back burner, until we were able to get rid of the monsters we had created.

During this time we forgot what a rib eye steak would taste like, but we became experts on making many forms of meat loaf. We learned how to stretch the family budget, or else.

Our relationships with other adults began to change. Sure, we retained the friends we had from the good old days, but we found they had moved to the far corners of the earth. There were a couple of wars in this time frame, to include World War II, the Korean conflict, and the Vietnam conflict. Men and women were scattered around the world during those years. During these war eras, women were often left home to tend to the children. It was difficult for them to find friendships unless they were involved in the labor force, the church, or the schools in which they had children enrolled.

World War II produced the most number of female workers. Women worked in factories, aircraft assembly lines, and sundry other places of work. It was not as crucial in the later conflicts for women to work. It did become increasingly necessary for women to work to keep food on the table. It was the norm in the past years for the women to work to provide a half of the family income. In 1998, 30 percent of the wives were the primary bread winners.

Social life often centered around the churches. Here one could find friends with similar interests. The public school system provided sources of social life for women involved in the PTA, or similar organizations.

As time went by, the youngsters began to leave the nest. This event was met with mixed emotions. Have you ever noticed how slowly sound travels? Sometimes the things you told your children when they were younger did not reach them until they were in their twenties.

Suddenly, the children left the home. Your gang you had in your youth was traded for a pair that produced a brood. You have gone the full circle. It can be perhaps better explained on the next page.

Our Sociological Voyage

As children we run in gangs.

At adolesence we begin to pair off.

Then we experience the empty nest syndrome.

We re-group and often (but not always) run in a gang again. If you do not believe it, go to a restaurant during the Winter Texan Season in the Valley.

We run the gauntlet from our early years to our "challenging" years.

Everybody loves a challenge.

The difference between "Winter Texans" and other older people becomes more clear. Although this chapter explains our journey through life, there is a difference in many aging people and the people who migrate to the warmer areas.

It is necessary to consider those who yet have mates, and those who have lost their mate. People often live differently in the two specific categories.

People who have lost a mate tend to "hole up" and stay home. They have invested so much of their time with a mate that they have to learn how to fly solo. In many such situations the widowed, women in particular, become reclusive in nature.

Couples often tend to draw within themselves and enjoy little social life with others. This is the difference between the motives of Winter Texans, as opposed to those who wish to stay at home during the hard winters.

Winter Texans want to get out of the cold weather and in doing so find themselves enveloped in a new society. They find new friends, largely because of the close proximity of their neighbor's housing.

Winter Texans live in tight quarters. If they live inland, or on the Island, they will live in condominiums, mobile homes, or motor homes. Few live in spacious homes.

In some parks there is so much to do as a group that one cannot easily be reclusive in nature. In later chapters you will read of the many, and varied housing options available to the Winter Texans.

So, if someone tells you Winter Texans are "different", believe them.

Chapter Two

Adieu Nomenclature To A New One
(Or)
From " Snow Birds" to "Winter Texans"

Thirty years ago people from the cold regions began to migrate to the Rio Grande Valley. They came, often pulling old travel trailers behind their cars. There were few places to park these vintage trailers so they parked them wherever they could find a suitable spot.

Many of these northerners were to find their way to South Padre Island to deposit their home on wheels on the sand dunes north of the little community. It was no easy chore to drag the trailers across the old bridge, but that is just what they did. The new bridge was not to be built until 1974. Prior to that time, the drivers had to go across to Long Island, then across the old bridge.

In later years, some trailer spaces became available within the city limits of South Padre Island, but when Cameron County officials decided to build a park on the southern tip of the Island, the creation of new spaces in the town came to a halt. Many "Snow Birds" simply moved to the north of the town . In time, they took advantage of the newer amenities to the south.

During this time, a new name was given to these folks from the cold country, "Winter Texans." There are as many accounts of the new name as there are people in the Valley. The name stuck, and those people who come down for the cold months are called by those two words.

You will see these people all over the Valley, from the Island to far to the western part of the Valley. Often, you can read their caps, or their name tags to determine where they live. At first thought, the identification appears to be a great way to advertise the park. Matter-of-fact, one wonders why people would wish to let you know from which park they have come.

There is a reason. In the event of an accident, or major health situation, the police will immediately look at your wallet to find out where you live. If you are not conscious, it might well appear you are from somewhere way up north. In extreme cases, the police might try to contact a spouse who is in fact sitting on the porch two blocks away. It is a safety measure that many park managers encourage. (The free advertisement is just an added perk to the program.)

Times have changed. The old trailers have been replaced by new and modern homes on wheels. There are fifth wheelers, simple pull behind you types, as well as motor homes that are not only luxury on wheels, but heavy on the pocket book.

Too, many Winter Texans buy lots on which to park their rigs each year. Others buy condominiums, largely on South Padre Island, in which to spend the cold times of the year.

A large number of these folks rent condominiums on the same Island, and come back year after year to the same compound. They develop relationships with other Winter Texans, and during the rest of the year, they maintain contact with their new associates.

The name change from "Snow Birds" to "Winter Texans" may change again. One would rather doubt it, but when you hear it you will get an inkling of the drift.

When my wife and I were shopping in Progreso, Mexico, a nice community to visit, we heard one of the venders explain that there were a whole bunch of "QTips" coming in their direction. We had never heard this term before, especially in reference to people.

When we asked the shop keepers why they referred to shoppers as "QTips", they replied, "Señor, do you not see the people coming with white hair and white shoes?"

How can you let a description like that get away?

"Well, there go the QTips."

If a person is ultra sensitive some of the humor in the descriptions of QTips might not set well. Normally, these older people have an unusual ability to laugh at themselves. After as many years as many have lived, and as many stories as they have heard, "maturing" people are flexible.

Michael Stephensen, who writes for many Valley newspapers, often uses his entire column for humor. He can be called a QTip or Winter Texan. He comes from Canada and spends six months out of the year in the Valley with his wife, Sally. Perhaps his humor is too much for Sally, for when Kathy and I met her she was on a bus with her mother, headed for Monterrey. She came back. After meeting these nice people I began to read more of Michael's writings. Here are some classics.

Sammy went to the doctor and complained, "I can't pee." "How old are you?" the doctor asked. "I'm 92." "You've peed enough."

Winter Texans are people who find that their children and their clothes are about the same age. And speaking of children, something I really like about children who visit the park- they don't go around showing pictures of their grandparents.

Two old friends met in beautiful downtown Weslaco and one invited the other to dinner. She gave directions to her park. "I'm in mobile 241", she said. "Just lean on the doorbell with your elbow." "Why should I use my elbow?" "You weren't coming empty-handed were you?"

Michael and Sally will be back this next cold season.

There are a number of bits of vocabulary known only by Winter Texans. An outsider would have difficulty in understanding the terms.

A Rumble: Twenty Qtips gather at a restaurant, take out their hearing aids, and leave their hats on at the table. The name of the game is to get those with the most hearing difficulties to sit at opposite ends of the table.

A Novice QTip: These are the new kids on the block who have not yet learned the most inexpensive places to live. (It takes at least one season.) These people even pay full retail costs for their clothing and food. In conversations, one couple will explain in detail the wonderful price they got on their condo rent for the season. Another couple will make a quick visit to the manager to see if there are other bargains available.

A Negotiator: This type will explain that the prices on living sites are excessive. They are quick to explain that they are living on a fixed income. (Perhaps they fail to understand almost everyone lives on a fixed income.)

Bingo: This is a game with numbered balls and cards that people hold while they are awaiting the bowls of popcorn. Often the visitors come only after the popcorn is being served.

Tour Group: Many travel companies offer bus tours into various parts of Mexico. Winter Texans love to ride the buses, chat with others and eat snacks they have hidden in their purses. Some actually listen to the historical lectures and look at the new scenery.

The Acceptable Imbibers: These folks love to have their drinks at the end of the day, say 5:00 P.M. Since happy hour starts at that time, many use Eastern Standard Time, though they live in Central Standard Time. Rules are rules!

The Hustlers: This is a fun game where people go to a favorite restaurant to eat. While they are eating, they commonly call for more bread. When they have carefully filled their purses and pockets with bread, they ask for bread to eat during the meal.

Stalkers: Most vacation establishments have fewer lounge chairs by the pool than they have people in the establishment. The stalkers watch from afar and grab a chair when someone leaves to get a coke. The real pros arrive an hour early to get the chairs.

The Decision Makers: In many vacation parks there is an array of activities, normally centered around food. The decision maker is the one who decides to head for the soup luncheon, the donut table, or the ice cream mid-afternoon snack. It is well to arrive one hour early at each function.

Big Dish Pros: It stands to reason that the bigger the dish you take to a pot-luck, the more you can get on the first run through the line.

Sweetener Bandits: For some reason people get the strange urge to slip little packets of sweeteners in their pockets. They take them home and deposit them in a special drawer in their kitchen. This goes on all season long, and the drawer gets to overflowing with the little packets. After the Qtips go home, the treasure of packets is returned to the restaurants.

Beach Runners: Let them tell you the fun of driving on the beach on South Padre Island. Probably one of every two drivers get stuck. If you do not have a four wheel drive, proceed with caution.

Hot Tub Testers: These are the few who constantly complain that the temperature in the hot tub is either too hot, or too cold.

The Buffet Gang: This set of terms apply to those who go through a buffet line and place one piece of food on their plate, the second in a bag in their purse, and etc. etc. , until enough is collected for the week.

Diet Freaks: These are the ones who are going to drive back north and immediately go on a diet. No one knows what happens.

If you are going to enjoy your stay in the Valley, you need to get accustomed to the particular language of the QTips. If you do not, you will be left in the dark much of the time.

When your park or condo rental agencies ask for someone to be contacted in case of an emergency, write down, " A good doctor."

A few spend a lot of time reading their Bibles. They are cramming for their finals.

Winter Texans have fun, even in the golden years. They come to the Valley for a good time in the sun and they do just that.

I was thinking about old age and decided that it is when you still have something on the ball but you are just too tired to bounce it.

Perhaps Winter Texans are not rich. Consider Henry Ford who never owned a Cadillac.

Chapter Three

Multifarious Species Propagate Trouble
(Or)
10% Cause 90% Of The Problems

Take this test.
    a. I bought this book at market price.
    b. I borrowed this book from my neighbor.
    c. I stole this book from my neighbor.
    d. I checked out this book at the library.
    e. I failed to return the book to the library.

If you answered "yes" to a or d, you are sure in the 90% of people who cause no problems. If you answered "yes" for b, you might be a border case. If you answered "yes" to c or e, you belong to the 10% of the people who cause 90% of the trouble.

    Yes, there are conflicts when thousands of Snow Birds, Winter Texans, or QTips, whatever the name, suddenly enter the Valley. It would be the same if thousands of Valley people suddenly settled in a northern part of the United States. It is hard to quickly assemble various groups together and plant them in a new territory.

    As QTips we must ask ourselves if we are among the 10 or 90 percent group. Too, as Valley natives, we are best advised to ask ourselves if we are in the 10 or 90 percent of the group.

    There are differences in folks from varied locations.

The element of "change" most often causes grief to people. When a quiet area is filled with new people, one experiences change. There are mixed reactions to this thing called change.

After going to the barber every month and getting right in, suddenly one finds himself sitting among a dozen men ahead of him in line. This causes anxiety and promotes prejudice. Why are these men here? Why do I have to sit here waiting for a haircut?

On the other hand, the barber is smiling all the way to the bank. QTips spend money in the Valley. The barbers and business owners like that extra money. To local residents it is like "having your mother-in-law drive off a five hundred foot cliff in your new Cadillac."

Yes, you will see bumper stickers that express some irritation. The Winter Texan has a sticker saying, WE ARE SPENDING OUR KID'S INHERITANCE, and a local will have one saying, I AM GOING TO GO UP NORTH AND DRIVE 20 MILES AN HOUR.

In most cases this is a light hearted feeling held by both the locals and the QTips. When you read the statistics in a later chapter, you will soon appreciate both sides of the coin.

Despite all the chatter, local residents like the visitors and the visitors like the local people. Again, there is change involved. The older we get the more reluctant we are to accept change.

In spite of all this, it is well to return to the 10 percent/ 90 percent formula. It is true that a small percentage of people on both sides cause difficulty.

This is true in almost any part of our society. If you live in a condominium you will always find one or more owners or renters who simply have to run the show. If you attend church board meetings you will find that one or two of the faithful are always at odds with the rest of the board. You can count in it! Having spent some thirty years as a counselor in the military establishment, I soon learned the 10 percent / 90 percent rule.

QTips and local residents are no different. It may be it is only a 5 percent / 95 percent ratio. You have encountered it in the park in which you live for a few months. Most often you will encounter difficult people on a tour bus. When the bus is ready to roll, the question comes up, "Where is Willy?"

Perhaps that is what makes this old world go around. Do gas prices go up when the folks from the northern regions need to fill their motor home? Probably so, in perhaps 5 percent of the cases. Do food prices go up during the QTip season? There may well be a few stores who take advantage of visitors. Of course, in doing so, they also take advantage of those who live in the Valley on a permanent basis. If you see an abuse, get hold of the right 10 percent of the locals and they will see to it that there is change.

The remainder of this book will deal with the positive aspects of our joint ventures. It is necessary to get the problem areas behind us to better focus on the nice relationships people have during the Winter Texan season.

It is well the locals get along with the QTips. Next year the QTips may become our permanent neighbors.

Chapter Four

Insular/ Indigenous Personnel Tethered
(Or)
QTips and Locals Work Well Together

There are many things that locals and visitors have in common. They agree that there are some needs in the community, as well as dire needs below the border. All of us share a need to be of assistance whenever we can. This takes place in common charities, the churches, and the synagogues. There is a common bond that keeps most people working together for good causes.

Churches are a place where people meet throughout the Valley. Attendance soars during the months of December, January, February, March, and even into April. Many churches, with smaller numbers of members, rely on the Winter Texans to keep the congregations afloat during the dry seasons.

It is well to use as an example, a religious organization about which I know the most, The Chapel By The Sea, on South Padre Island. Most similar groups in the Valley share in the cooperation of QTips, but because I have attended this Chapel for several years, I can more ably relate the cooperation, and fun, that goes on at this particular place. It is but one example of the sundry religious organizations that truly appreciate the worshippers from the cold country.

The Chapel is a multi-denominational organization where worshippers from all over the Valley gather for morning services. During most of the year there is but one service at 8:30 A.M. When the QTips arrive, the Chapel provides three services to take care of the crowds. Many Valley people like to attend services at this Chapel, go to brunch, and play on the Island the rest of the day. The dress is "casual."

There are no members at this Chapel, and there is no intent to have any members. The congregation comes from a vast menu of denominations, normally from within the Christian community. It is a great chance to sit by a Lutheran, if you are a Baptist, or a Methodist, if you are a Catholic.

Bob Hope was at the airport to meet his wife, Dolores, who was flying in after doing some charity work for the Catholic Church. When her private plane pulled in, they put the steps down. The first two people off the plane were Catholic priests, then came Dolores, and then came four more priests. Hope nudged a friend and said, "I don't know why she just doesn't buy insurance like everybody else."

Winter Texans fill the Chapel, with attendance reaching almost one thousand people during the peak seasons. The same people serve coffee to others, assist in squeezing people into the sanctuary, as well as helping with other needed chores.

A lady married a man who was wealthy. A friend asks, "Did you marry him for his money?" "Not at all", she replied, "but it is nice." We like the QTips, as well as the financial support they provide.

You know when people see a cat's litter box, they always say, "Oh, have you got a cat?" Just once I wanted to say, "No, it's for company."

When you turn to your right after crossing onto the Island, you can drive a few blocks and just prior to entering the county park, look for a sign on your left . You do not need to enter the park entrance. Turn left when you see the sign, Chapel By The Sea.

This Chapel is not for company. It's for you. It was built to serve a tiny community and a vast migration of people from the snow country. You will find friends from every part of the United States and a lot of Canada.

If you arrive in December, you may take part in a Christmas tradition at the Chapel. Each year, the Boys and Girls Club of Port Isabel become the sponsors for youngsters who have less. This group asks various organizations and churches to provide gifts for those who would otherwise get very few, if any, gifts.

The congregation at the Chapel provides a large tree under which attendees can place gifts for children. It is a sight to behold, and rumor is that the Chapel gives more than any other organization to this worthy cause.

The minister often asks the congregation, by a show of hands, where they are from, and the denomination to which they belong. This helps develop a great deal of "partnership" for people away from their home church. (Although most of them secretly are happy that they are down in the Valley, away from the ice and snow, perhaps they pray for those back home.)

When you attend, arrive early to get a place to sit.

In 1998, a new book was published for the people interested in the Chapel. It is entitled "Chapel By The Sea." This became a joint effort of local residents and Winter Texans. The front cover was painted by Mr. Gene Washburn, the manuscript was prepared by Mrs. Connye Busa, the illustrations were drawn by Mr. Tommy Carruth, with a lot of technical help from Dr. Milton Messinger.

The cost to the Chapel came to $6.50 a book. When the book came on the "contribution market" it was not unusual to see contributions of up to $110.00 per book from the QTips. They do as much, hopefully, in the many churches throughout the Valley.

A well worn dollar bill and a similarly destressed twenty arrived at the Bureau of Engraving and Printing to be retired. As they moved along the conveyor belt to the shredder they struck up a conversation. The twenty dollar bill reminisced about its travel all over the country.

"I've been to Las Vegas and Atlantic City, the finest restaurants in New York, performances on Broadway, and even a cruise from Miami."

"Wow!", said the single bill, "you really have gotten around." " So tell me", says the twenty, "where have you been throughout your lifetime?"

"Oh, I've been to the Methodist Church, the Charismatic Church, the Baptist Church, the Lutheran Church.........."

And the twenty asks, "What's a church?"

Oh yes, QTips have a great deal of humor. Where did you think this story got its start?

QTips appear to be quite religious in nature. The churches are full when these folks are in the Valley. One wrote, asking for a place for a spiritual retreat.

A new Winter Texan wrote to a campground about a week's vacation. Uppermost in her mind were the accomodations for the bathroom facilities. Too proper to write "toilet", she abbreviated "B.C." for bathroom commode. She asked if the campground had its own "B.C."

The campground staff, baffled by the use of "B.C.", asked around but no one knew what it meant. Someone finally said, "Oh, she means the Baptist Church! She's asking if the campground has its own Baptist Church."

The manager sat down and wrote:

Dear Madam:

I am sorry about the delay in answering your letter, but I am pleased to tell you that there is a a B.C. nine miles north of the campground and is capable of sitting 250 people. I admit it is quite a distance away but if you are in the habit of going regularly, you will be pleased to know a good many people go and take their lunches with them and spend the day. They usually arrive early and stay late.

The last time my wife and I went was six years ago and it was so crowded we had to stand up the whole time we were there. It may interest you to know there is a supper planned to raise money to buy more seats.

I would like to say it pains me greatly to not be able

to go more regularly, but it is surely no lack of desire on my part. As we grow older it seems to be more of an effort, especially in cold weather.

If you desire to come to our campground, I can go with you the first time, sit with you, and introduce you to all the folks. Please remember this is a friendly community.

    Sincerely,
        Your new friends

Rumor has it that a retired QTip minister was asked to fill in at a Valley church. He was very nervous after being out of the pulpit so long. He conferred with a younger RGV pastor. The younger one advised the retired man to have a glass of vodka at the pulpit, and when he became nervous, just take a sip. The young man even offered to critique the presentation.

After the service, the young minister explained:
1. Next time, "sip" rather than "gulp."
2. There are ten commandments, not twelve.
3. There are twelve Disciples, not ten.
4. We <u>do not</u> refer to the cross as the "Big T."
5. David slew Goliath, he did not kick the . . . . out of him.
6. The Father, Son and Holy Spirit are <u>never</u> called "Big Daddy, Junior, and Spook."
7. The recommended prayer at the pot-luck lunch is not, "Rub-A-Dub-Dub, thanks for the grub. Yeah God."

    This did not happen at the Chapel By The Sea.

In addition to the QTip involvement with various churches and synagogues, these "frozen chosen" do a lot for the Rio Grande Valley.

If you visit a library, you will most often find at least one helping at the desk, or dusting off the shelves. Visit a hospital and you will see men and women at work on a volunteer basis, perhaps to keep busy, but more probably, to help the sick.

RGV public school systems are most appreciative of the professional help they get. When schools in various parts of America are graduating students who cannot read, much help is needed. Let us emphasize something.

Retired People Have Much To Offer This Younger Generation

(I said it and I'm glad. I feel good all over.)

There is a myth that older people have little to offer this world. This is not only a myth, but a sad commentary by the uninformed. Mature adults still have minds, some holding graduate degrees on their walls, while others have expertise in a thousand different vocations. Some senior citizens even write books after the scary age of sixty-five. There is a reason for the larger size print in this book.

Winter Texan quilters make comfortable quilts for youngsters who must leave the homes of abusive parents. (I had to mention this --- my wife is a quilter.)

An interesting story going around the Valley is about a lady named Jo Bauer, who is called "Mama Candy" at the Casa Amparo orphanage in Reynosa.

According to the story, Jo and her husband Bill, spend a great deal of time at the orphanage and help with fund raising activities such as barbecues and rummage sales.

The home, under the supervision of Sister Natividad, provides shelter and food for children, from age eighteen months to 20 years old, who have no living parents, or who have run away from home.

Of course Jo always takes candy to the children, and gained the above name.

Other Winter Texans joined in and helped improve the old building, with broken windows, leaking roofs, with no hot water. Helen Menendez started a typing class to give the youngsters a skill, while her husband Everett works with the electrical and plumbing jobs.

Another Winter Texan, Harold Sitzmann, took on the job of hauling beds and mattresses to Casa Amparo.

There is the strong probability that when these QTips go back to their homes in the spring, they have some very similar projects there. People who practice charity in the Valley are prone to do the same wherever they go.

An interesting observation is that people who do not get involved in helping others are the same ones who complain about the place they live, the few bad days that are going to come around, and the unfriendly couple down the street. Sitting in the sun around the pool is fun, but it can also get old .

There is no doubt that local residents and QTips do work together. At a restaurant, the owner will let you do the ordering, and he will relieve you of your money

Winter Texans have been known to do a lot of community labor for the Valley. They have been involved in "Keep Texas Clean" programs, as well as the "Keep Our Beaches Clean" programs.

Sure, a few QTips and local residents trash the beach. A new law is now in effect that will cost either party a bundle if caught dropping litter on the beach. The enforcement people <u>mean business,</u> the fines are very high and one can go to jail.

There are reasons for this new emphasis on beach-trashing. Two years ago, some 1100 workers picked up approximately 21.49 <u>tons</u> of litter. QTips did their part in that effort as well.

Basic to all this, both Winter Texans and local residents have their share of adjustments and problems. When adjustments are necessary, a degree of anxiety is produced. QTips are living in smaller quarters than their home back in the colder regions. Trailer parks are different.

A Child's View of Retirement in a Mobile Home Park

The teacher asked her small pupils how they spent their holiday. One of the boy's reply went like this. "We visit Grandma and Grandpa each year. They used to live up here in a big brick house, but Grandpa got retarded and they moved to Texas. They live in a park with a lot of other retarded people. They all live in tin huts. They ride tricycles that are too big for me. They all go to a building called the wrecked hall, but is fixed now. They all exercise but not very well. There is a swimming pool but I guess nobody teaches them; they just stand around with their hats on.

My Grandma used to bake cookies for me, but nobody cooks down there. They all go to restaurants that are fast and have discounts. When you come into the park, there is a doll house with a man sitting in it. He watches all day so they can't get out without him seeing them. I guess everybody forgets who they are because they all wear badges with their names on them.

Grandma says Grandpa worked hard all his life to earn his retardment. I wish they would move back home, but I guess the man in the doll house won't let them out."

Even local people have adjustments. When a local moves into a condominium, he really has adjustments.

The Condo Association

The first lesson in condo living begins with a visit from the condo association president who has a lot of time on his hands because his wife works to keep food on the table. He is elected on a platform of leadership.

Of course he ran unopposed, because nobody else wanted the job. But now he's president for life. **That's because it is his life!**

He issues orders, makes up petty rules and polices the parking lot for cigarette butts. He let's you know if your car is parked outside the yellow lines, if it's dripping oil on the parking lot, or if it needs waxing.

You can escape him by hiding out at the pool, but you had better go early if you want a chair. Each day many of the condo residents wake up at 6:00 A.M., hurry down to the pool, and place large beach towels on the lounge chairs to reserve them for later use. One of the first unwritten laws you need to learn at any condo is that towels indicate possession.

During the first month the new resident will probably attend a condo association meeting, "just to protect the few rights you've got left."

At this meeting you will get acquainted with the lady in 204 who is keeping a dog in her condo, even though it is a clear violation of the rules. She will make the case that her dog is 15 years old and has only a few good months left. Her appeal will be tabled, as it has been for the past four years.

You'll be introduced to the widow in 601 who grabs your arm, squeezes your hand, and invites you up to her condo for a little drink after the meeting.

And you'll meet the condo manager, who takes you aside and tells you why he needs a raise in salary.

But don't despair. You can always find refuge on your 3 X 6 foot balcony, as long as it's not overlooking all those towel-covered lounge chairs at the pool!

Every person, be it a QTip or a permanent local, has adjustments to Valley living. Take your troubles, then add the many other troubles to the guy on the other side of the coin, and you can understand that, despite what people often imply, Winter Texans and locals get along very well.

Chapter Five

Where Insular Earthlings Inhabit
(Or)
Some Communities Where QTips Stay

Winter Texans begin arriving in the Rio Grande Valley as early as November and many stay through the month of March. Certainly, some come only for the months of January and February. A few couples stay but one month.

They enter the Valley boundaries, difficult to define, and begin their search for a place to land. They often come equipped with suggestions from veterans of former journeys and in many cases have already made reservations for their stay.

Yes, some go to South Padre Island, where there are facilities for both mobile units and condominiums. Others stop short of that longer trail and find comfortable lodging in many parts of the RGV.

In this chapter, you can get a quick view of some of the major "haunts" of these QTips. It would appear a bit difficult to mention each and every town, as well as the hundreds of settlement sites.

To get an idea of possibilities, this chapter can contain some of the places where QTips settle.

Mission, Texas

Mission was established in 1824 by the Oblate Fathers on a site three miles south of the present town. The priests planted the first orange trees, with the result that today this town is the home of the original citrus empire in the RGV.

The town boasts some 28,618 residents, (except when the QTips reside there for a few months.) A large number of these winter visitors live in and around Mission.

Each December, the town hosts the annual "Tropical Christmas." The Poinsettia flower is the center of this attraction. It is worth the drive to see these flowers.

About three miles south, you can visit Anzalduas Park, on the Rio Grande. There are rest rooms, birding piers, boat docks, and paved roads.

Probably the most interesting site for many is the Los Ebanos Ferry, the only existing hand-operated ferry on the Rio Grande. This ferry is about fifteen miles from Mission.

There are many RV parks in this community. They are found in abundance and some say the area around Mission grows up to 15 percent in population during the Winter Texan season.

Do take the time to visit La Lomita Chapel, first built in 1865. It is the site of an overnight way station once used by Oblate priests on horseback, who traveled the Valley, spreading their faith.

Weslaco, Texas

The name comes from the initials of W.E. Steward Land Company, that promoted the town site in 1919.

The city hall, built in 1928, features intricate cast stone sculpture adorning the entryway. The interior is decorated with Spanish tiles in geometric designs.

The Bicultural Museum holds artifacts from the daily lives of the region's Hispanic and Anglo settlers.

The Valley Tourist Information Center provides a great amount of information for travelers, visitors, and QTips.

Too, it might be well to visit the Weslaco Tourist Information Center. You can learn about local attractions, and accommodations throughout the Valley.

Rumor has it that Weslaco is most appreciative of the efforts of the Winter Texans to contribute time and effort to local worthy causes.

Another good thing about this area is that it is within a close driving range to Nuevo, Progreso. Everyone visits that small town. On one day in 1998, over 20,000 people visited that small shopping community. There is more about that Mexican town in a later chapter.

A visitor was asking about the population of Weslaco. The longtime resident began to think about it. Finally he replied, "Most of the time we must have around 23,000 people, except during the winter when we must have close to 30,000 residents." "You know," he continued, " those people are OK."

Travel Stories

A woman called and said, "I need to fly to Pepsi-Cola on one of those computer planes." I asked if she meant to fly to Pensacola on a commuter plane." She said, "Yea, whatever."

A client called in inquiring about a package to Hawaii. After going over the cost info, she asked, "Would it be cheaper to fly to California and then take a train to Hawaii?"

A nice lady just called. She needed to know how it was possible that her flight from Detroit left at 8:20am and got into Chicago at 8:33am. I tried to explain that Michigan was an hour ahead of Illinois, but she could not understand the concept of time zones. Finally I told her the plane went very fast, and she bought that.

I just got off the phone with a man who asked, "How do I know which plane to get on?" I asked him exactly what he meant, which he replied, "I was told my flight number is 823, but none of these darn planes have numbers on them."

A man called, furious about a Florida package we had put together. "You promised me an ocean view in Orlando. I know Orlando is in the middle but I looked on the map and it is a thin state."

Brownsville, Texas

This city began in 1846 when General Zachary Taylor established Fort Brown to confirm the Rio Grande as the national boundary after Texas became a U.S. State. During most of the year, the population stays at around 100,000, until the QTips swell the population figures.

Brownsville is the Valley's largest city, situated on the Rio Grande in a subtropical part of Texas. If you, while driving, come to a large bridge, be sure that you are leaving the United States and entering Mexico.

While staying in this city, you would be advised to visit the following sites of interest:

Brazos Island State Park - Located about 22 miles east of the city, you can swim, fish, or just enjoy the Gulf of Mexico. This is not a developed site with all the facilities you will find on South Padre Island.

Gladys Porter Zoo - This zoo is without bars and cages. Rare exotic animals are displayed in natural settings.

Historic Brownsville Museum - A lot of history in pictures and documents of local interest, housed in the Southern Pacific Depot.

The list of things to do and see can go on and on. This city is a good one to visit when you have at least an entire day at your disposal. You might need more time to get everything done.

Donna, Texas

Almost everyone has heard of, or has seen a building called the "American Legion." This worthy organization has been a part of the American scene for many years. In Donna, Texas you will be able to visit the oldest American Legion Hall in the United States.

Donna is a haven for hundreds of QTips. The town, boasting a population of nearly 12,000 people, has always opened its arms to those from the north.

Donna was founded on the St. Louis, Brownsville, and Mexico Railroad in 1906.

Donna Hooks was the daughter of a townsite promoter. It was from this name that the community got its identity.

Donna is a retail center for the ranching and agriculture efforts of the Rio Grande Valley. It has opened its boundaries to special winter guests.

Donna Hooks Fletcher Museum -

Here you will find memorabilia, photographs, and artifacts from the days of the town's founding. Too, you will see the restored bar of the early day "Blue Goose Saloon." All of this, and more, is housed in the historic American Legion Hall, built in 1920.

McAllen, Texas

Ask almost any Winter Texan the place they find more welcome than McAllen, and you will hear little in the way of response. It has been named "the casual town" by visitors from Canada and the northern plains.

You will see people strolling in slacks and sport shirts, among the blossoming citrus groves. Tourist parks cater to these people with dances, tours, bridge, domino and shuffleboard tournaments. There are many concerts and shows for the winter visitors.

"Tourism" is a big part of the economy of McAllen. They know a good thing when they see it. Too, there is an emphasis on gas, oil, citrus products, and international trade with Mexico.

McAllen International Museum -
Here one can view Mexican art, colorful masks and costumes in the Ethnography Gallery. View geology, archeology, and mineral specimens in the Earth Science Gallery.

Reynosa, Mexico -
Visit a thriving city of some 250,000 people, just eight miles south of McAllen, just across the Rio Grande River. This is a tourist town, with fine foods, many forms of art work, and every so often, bullfights.

Perhaps this is the place where two worlds meet. In a few minutes you can be transformed from the American way of doing things, to the Mexican way of life.

San Juan, Texas

Maybe you have driven around the valley and have noticed open ditches that permit water to be diverted to irrigate crops. Too, you may have seen large cement pipes through which water runs.

Perhaps you have never been real interested in just where the pipes were manufactured, but you will learn now that the large portion of the pipes are made in the town of San Juan.

(Another question you had but hesitated to ask.)

San Juan was organized in 1909, close to the Missouri Pacific railroad. The town was named after John Closner but the name of San Juan was to become the official, although Spanish name.

As you drive near this community you can see the roads lined with scarlet bougainvillea.

The town, boasting some 9000 residents, is a haven for many Winter Texans. The community appreciates the visitors and on one day each year they sponsor a "pick a grapefruit day" for these visitors.

In 1954, the Shrine of La Virgen de San Juan del Valle, was completed. The edifice contained many imported works of art,

The structure was burned to the ground after it was hit by an airplane. (Rumor is that it was a deliberate act.) The crash in 1970 spared the wooden statue of Our Lady of San Juan, now housed in a five million dollar shrine, paid for by small donations.

Rio Hondo, Texas

Rio Hondo is a small town of some 2000 people, situated on the bank of the Arroyo Colorado. The community is spread along the waterway. Winter Texans speak of the "easy going" population and the local friendships they make . It does not hurt that the temperatures are very favorable.

In 1910, a few land promoters conducted a contest to pick a name for the little town. The name was selected which means "deep river." In 1927 the town was incorporated.

In the downtown area you will find a vintage drug store that yet holds an old soda fountain, now a part of history.

A large lift-span bridge is in the middle of the town. Barges, going from the Gulf to the Port of Harlingen, carry cargo on this deep body of water.

There is a party-boat cruise offered that will take you from the Port of Harlingen to the Laguna Madre.

Texas Air Museum

Some 100 people who were interested in aviation formed this museum. The work is still in progress, and it can be assumed that the museum will always be a continuing project. One can visit aircraft not found in other museums, and enjoy the friendship of the locals who have dedicated themselves to this project.

Port Isabel, Texas

The more prominent structure you will see when you are in this community is the old lighthouse and the light house keepers home. The home was completed to exact detail of the original in 1997. The lighthouse, at the time of this writing, is being repaired.

In 1850, the congress approved the expenditure of $15,000 to build the lighthouse. The plans called for the structure to be twenty feet in diameter at the base, gradually tapering to twelve feet at the top.

On March 20, 1853, the light was turned on. During the Civil War the light was turned off by the Confederate command, only to be turned on again by the Union troops.

The town was first named El Fronton de Santa Isabella, when it was established in the 1828. In 1849 the town was named Point Isabel, and is normally called Port Isabel at this time.

The town boasts over 4000 residents. It is the last town you will enter prior to your journey across the long bridge to South Padre Island. At a length of three miles, it is the longest bridge in Texas.

Fishing is great in this area. It is also the home of one of the largest shrimp fleets in the world, and many restaurants to serve shrimp in a dozen ways you will appreciate.

Do not fail to visit the newest Valley Museum in the Champion Building. This is a must for anyone who is interested in the history of the Valley.

Take A Break!
(Retirees need to learn how to take a break and not feel guilty about it.)

Favorite Hymns

Dentist's Hymn
"Crown Him With Many Crowns"
The TV Weatherman's Hymn
"There Shall Be Showers of Blessings"
The Contractor's Hymn
"The Church's One Foundation"
The Tailor's Hymn
"Holy, Holy, Holy"
The Golfer's Hymn
"There Is a Green Hill Far Away"
The Politician's Hymn
"Standing On The Promises"
The Optometrist's Hymn
"Open My Eyes That I May See"
The Gossiper's Hymn
"Pass It On"
The Electrician's Hymn
"Send Out Thy Light"
The Shopper's Hymn
"Sweet By and By"
The IRS Hymn
"All To Thee"
or
"I Surrender All"

Alamo, Texas

Visitors to this community of some 8,000 people speak well of the friendly people of the community. Many QTips stay in this area and enjoy the surrounding area. Named after the Alamo Sugar and Land Company, the town was incorporated in 1924.

Near Alamo one can visit the Santa Ana Wildlife Refuge, about 2,000 acres of land protected for the preservation of nature that existed in the beginning of time.

Too, Sutherland's Cactus Garden is worth visiting. It consists of 5 acres of native and exotic cacti.

The closeness of the Mexican border makes it handy to go shopping in Mexico, via U.S. 281.

Pharr, Texas

This community of 24,000 began when a sugar planter from Louisiana, named Henry N. Pharr, began operations in the vicinity. The town, incorporated in 1909, is named after him.

Visit the Old Clock Museum, and see over 450 clocks, some dating back to 1690, or visit the leather factory and watch items being made from leather. You are welcome at this factory.

Mexico is but 11 miles away, by using U.S. 281, as is true of Alamo. Many people retire in this warm area.

Edinburg, Texas

It is said that Winter Texans make up a large part of the population of 30,000 residents. The town began with the name, Chapin, the man who first promoted the area. In 1911, the name was changed to Edinburg.

Like other Valley communities, the area thrives on the citrus industry, along with many other crops of vegetables. The sunny area is good for agriculture.

Items of interest include the Hildago County Historical Museum, a nice lake, El Sal del Rey, and the Sheriff"s Posse Rodeo.

Los Fresnos, Texas

As you drive towards South Padre Island, you will drive through this growing area, some 20 miles from the Island.

Because of the fishing in the Laguna Madre area, many QTips park their mobile homes in this town. This affords them the luxury of being close to the bay, the beach, and all that goes with it.

In the past two years, highway 100 has been widened into a four lane road to the Island. One must go through Los Fresnos to get to the salty waters for boating, fishing, and swimming.

Perhaps this town provides quick access to the Gulf at prices somewhat lower than directly on the water.

Harlingen, Texas

There are tons of Winter Texans in Harlingen and the surrounding areas, like San Benito, just South of Harlingen. It might be said that this is the hub of the headquarters of the QTips.

On a following page you can read just a few of the many activities that are offered in this area. (Bear in mind, this is just a sample on page 41.)

Harlingen was incorporated in 1905, and currently boasts of a population of over 50,000, except during the winter when the number swells.

Do take the time to visit the Iwo Jima War Memorial, located at the Marine Military Academy, just two blocks from the airport.

The Laguna Atascosa National Wildlife Refuge is located some 25 miles East of the city. The refuge is made up of 7,000 acres of marsh, salt and fresh water, along with trees and brush for protection of migrating birds that land in the area.

Visit the Port of Harlingen and watch huge barges being moved down the Arroyo Colorado, headed for the Gulf of Mexico. Too, you can join others in a party boat that takes you down this deep river. You do not want to miss this experience.

There are hundreds of RV parks in this area, with more activities than most can handle. Winter Texans can stay as busy as they wish, according to the sample list on the next page.

Winter Texan Activities
(Just a few of many things to do, many of which I know nothing about)

Country Western Pattern Dance Class
Cribbage
Mainstream Square Dancing
Old Time Fun Dance
Euchre
Intermediate Clogging
Ballroom Dance Lessons
Woodcarving Workshop
Contra Dancing
Spaghetti Every Monday
(I can understand that one)
Beginners Country Western
Advanced Country Western
Hamburgers With Fixins
(Now we're talking)

Of course there are other things like traveling, fishing, visiting Mexico, swimming, walking the beach, or sitting in the sun creating skin cancer

Above all, do not come to the Valley to pass time. We just do not have that much time. True, we live much longer than our ancestors, but we need not die of boredom. Sitting in a group, gossiping, doesn't cut it.

On the other hand, as in "Fiddler On The Roof", if you wish to do nothing, it is your buck. Sit in the sun and be grateful that "wrinkles don't hurt."

South Padre Island, Texas

On a recent cruise to the West Indies, my wife and I explained to some new friends that we lived on South Padre Island. A lady exclaimed, "Oh, I have a cousin who lives in Corpus Christi, just across the bay."

Corpus Christi is wonderful. It is exciting. It can be romantic, but it is not across the bay from South Padre Island! South Padre Island is at the lowest tip of Texas, close to Brownsville.

In 1964, South Padre Island became a separate island from Padre Island. After the completion of the Port Mansfield Gulf Channel, the barrier reef South of the channel was named South Padre Island.

Now that we have that straight, you can inform your relatives that if they cross the causeway in Corpus Christi, they must turn back and drive three hours more to the South.

The island is a place where ties are not allowed. It is a place to relax and enjoy the surf, go fishing, or take part in many water sports. Some 1400 people live on the Island, until the QTips arrive and the numbers rise most dramatically.

Many people live in RV parks, and many rent condos from owners on the Island. Most rentals are found with local rental agencies.

The small Island is filled with excellent places to eat, and the typical QTip gains _____ pounds during their stay on the sandy reef. (You can fill in the space.)

The Island is a place to relax and find your own way of entertainment. As a resort community, it provides all the things you need, but you must determine what you wish to do.

As you drive South on U.S. 77, turn left on U.S.100 to get to the Island. If you miss it, you are in the Gulf of Mexico.

Relax and Enjoy

The time comes when the wisest thing to do is settle down and enjoy the advantages old age brings.

---You can take naps with no apologies and no feelings of guilt.
---You can say no to any number of requests for your services and time. ("I've already done that" is a response that works.)
---You can conveniently forget what you want to forget.
---It doesn't concern you one way or the other when mini-skirts make another comeback.
---You can initiate conversations with strangers and nobody questions your motives.

The Island is home to the aging generation for a few months, and then it comes to an abrupt end, when thousands of Spring Breakers swarm over the beaches, followed by the summer vacation crowd.

Sure, I used two pages to explain the Island, and only one page for other sites. I live on the Island and I am writing this book.

Just for grins, relax on the beach and wait for someone to walk by from your home town. It will happen. The Island is the meeting place for people from around the world. You will enjoy the warm sun, and the breeze coming off the Gulf of Mexico.

The short list of towns I have described falls short of listing all towns in the Valley. There are many smaller towns where you can find very adequate neighbors. Just a tip-- the average cost to park your RV in the RGV is a little less than $200 a month, for a full hook-up. As you go to the Island, you will see a rise in costs.

In the back portion of this book you will find the opportunity to list places you stay that I have missed. It is my hope that you will provide your views on the best RV parks in which to reside, the better places to eat, and the most enjoyable places to visit in the Valley.

In a later chapter you will be exposed to the Valley in a more general way, and this can assist you in making your selection for the best area to visit, or to stay for a few months.

If you are not in the "clip and write" mood, you can always leave information with me on the internet at ATibbetts @ AOL. Com. I solicit all the information I can get from you since this book can be published each year with the latest reports that are good. Probably, I will not record the "bad news" you might contribute about a RV park or a restaurant, simply because good news is always better.

It is always good to be positive. Remember that as people age they can tend to be negative. Being positive is the best cure for good health, along with an annual physical, good diet and a lot of exercise. Always remember, we pass this way only once--- unless your spouse is reading the road map.

Chapter Six

Que Haciastuen Mexico?
(Or)
What Do You Do In Mexico?

You may not believe this. but it is true. A friend drove me to Reynosa , Mexico to go to a dance in a downtown hotel ballroom. The room was crowded with QTips dancing and drinking margaritas, sold at half price. Everything was normal with one exception. The dance was held at 12:00 --**noon**. Let the party begin!

"We'll have to wrap this up before it gets dark."

There are a number of towns, communities, and cities just across the border into Mexico. Many of the RV parks are just a few miles from some of them. Perhaps much of the lure for people visiting the Valley is the close proximity to Mexico.

A favorite is the town of Progreso, Mexico. This was once a sleepy little town with a few stores to sell trinkets to the few Americans who visited. However, in the past years the town has developed into a rather large shopping area. They like QTips, and they depend on them for survival.

Perhaps it is best to park on the American side and walk the short distance to the shopping areas. During the busy season, it is often hard to get in and out of the town by car. Remember, this is the town where the description "QTips" began.

The venders are most polite, and you can feel safer in Progreso than in many American towns. Many visitors go for the sole purpose of buying medicine. As a general rule, any medicine produced in Mexico is a great deal less costly than what Americans are used to paying.

One can purchase many hand made crafts as well as some foods, and a variety of candy. You will find an assortment of bargains you simply have to own, even though you lack the space to store them. They do make good gifts for the people you left up North.

There are several excellent dining establishments in Progreso. The food (not off the streets) seems to be safe in the better restaurants.

The citizens of Nuevo Progreso appreciate your visits, and your money. They have a big celebration each year to express their gratitude to the Americans who come to visit, and spend money.

This year over 20,000 people swarmed the little town for the big party. They set up five large stages on the streets to play pop, rock'n'roll, and traditional Mexican folk music.

The town provided free drinks and food for this special Winter Texan Day. (These people from the cold country have noses that can pick up the scent of food and drinks from thirty miles away.)

Did you know you can buy a ROLEX watch for $20.00 in Progreso? Now who would be so dumb as to think one can purchase a watch that normally sells for thousands of dollars, for a mere $20.00? This is a test of our individual intelligence. It would take a very dumb person to buy such an impossible deal. It is often a hard thing to realize that people can be so slow in the brain attic. **However, the one I bought is still running.**

The real story was when a Progreso real estate guy sold a QTip the deed to Bagdad Island. The Island was a famous one in its day. It was a shipping port for cotton, and often called "sin city." Perhaps that caught his fancy.

However, little did he know that a hurricane hit the Brownsville area in 1844 and wiped out the Island. It is still there, under water, but no one knows just where.

When you go shopping, buyer beware!

Another city visited by thousands of Winter Texans is the city of Reynosa. This is no small town, and one can find about anything needed in this river town.

The Rio Grande River is a long, winding stream of water that begins in Colorado, high in the Rocky Mountains, then flows down through New Mexico and Texas. The cold, pure water of the river changes as it flows to the South, temporarily blocked by a series of man made dams, to include Elephant Butte Dam in New Mexico, with three more large dams downstream to hold back the water for irrigation of crops. As the river heads to its point of entry into the Gulf of Mexico, near Brownsville, Texas, it gets less and less pure or cold. Pollution takes its toll and it has been named by environmentalists to be one of the most polluted rivers in the United States.

The problem rests with the practice of allowing raw sewage and industrial waste to be dumped into its banks. By the time it gets to the Gulf, it is not fit to drink, and there have been reports of people dying who swam in the murky waters.

Reynosa rests in the northern Valley sector of this long river. With a population in excess of 300,000 people, it is possible that more waste is simply too much for the river to handle. The river has been collecting debris and unsafe garbage for hundreds of miles.

The city of Reynosa is an excellent place to visit. It is advised that you be very careful about the water you drink, due to the fact that the drinking water in the city comes from the Rio Grande River. BYOB.

As you cruise on down the Rio Grande River you will next see the city of Matamoros, Mexico. This too is a large city of several hundred thousand people. You can cross the river from Brownsville, or if you want a real thrill you can cross at Reynosa on Mexican Highway 40, then left on Mexican Highway 2, until you reach Matamoros. Some QTips want more thrills than others!

This city has had many names. Its present name came in 1823 in honor of Don Mariano Matamoros, a hero of Mexican independence. It was a seaport used by the Confederacy during the American Civil War.

Like the sister cities up the river, there is an abundance of bargains you cannot do without. You can save so much money you end up broke.

The streets are crowded and driving is for those with nerves of steel, or recent graduates of mental institutions. If you are from Detroit, Chicago, New York City, or a city of similar size, you will find this a lark to navigate, or you will end up in an institution.

Let us talk about drinking water in Mexico.

As a general rule, stay clear of any water unless an associate, who is not sick, tells you the water is safe at certain places. If you get Montezuma's Revenge , you listened to the wrong associate.

Americans are rather protected from dangerous water, and the result is that we do not build up immunity to the many diseases we can get from the drinking water in foreign countries. There may be some set rules for you to follow, but you will not get them from this writer.

It is possible to take tours, often by bus, into the interior of Mexico. There are several tour agencies who cater to QTips and local residents. You can read about tours in the Sunday local newspapers.

There are long tours taken by airplane, and by train. It seems there is an unending source of travel in the RGV.

Just One Example

Two months ago my wife, Kathy, myself and Harvey and Jackie Merrell decided to tour Monterrey, Mexico. We called a local agency and signed up. (Harvey is a retired owner of a car dealership so he knew how to sign a contract.)

As soon as we joined thirty others we found that some were QTips we knew from the Island. We also traveled with Sally Stephenson, the wife of Michael, who, as mentioned before, writes witty things about people in the Valley.

Depending on the particular tour, you can catch the bus at different locations. We picked Brownsville as our point of departure. We picked up people in some five towns before crossing into Mexico at Reynosa.

The bus was a very clean and modern Mercedes, with a driver and tour director. The vehicle was very comfortable with a rest room in the back.

We traveled to Monterrey, visited some delightful sights enroute, and after spending two nights, and many hours sight-seeing, we headed back for home.

The entire cost of transportation, excellent lodging, and some meals cost $160.00 a person.

There are other ways to see the Valley and Mexico. As for me, I am retired and do not want much responsibility when I travel. I like to let someone else do the driving, find a place to sleep, or select a good place to eat. My wife can go in either direction on this subject.

There is a couple on the Island, Gene and Dana Washburn, who are on the other side of the "fun fence." Gene is an international artist, who with Dana, travel a lot in Mexico on their own. They simply get into their vehicle and head south. To me, this is foreign, but my wife shares their idea of travel, and fortunately my ideas as well. My idea of adventure is calling for coffee when I get out of bed on a cruise. Kathy shares her notes from a journey to La Pesca, Mexico with Dana and Gene. We can do without the grammar and stuff, to just get her facts.

Left Brownsville about noon for La Pesca, 200 miles down the coast. Highway 70 to La Pesca rough some of the way with chug holes. Got to La Pesca about 6:30. Turned right on first street past bridge. Passed a new church and a new cafe, not yet open, to a restaurant and two-story motel in back. Ate a fresh trout dinner, fried potatoes, sliced tomatoes and onions, tortillas, and a coke. (Fresh shrimp appetizer) Cost $3.20.

Rented a room that night for $6.00 per person. Ceiling fan and hot water.

Up early to a breakfast of eggs, toast, refried beans and coffee for $2.50 We drove to the beach and hired a fisherman to take us across the river where we shelled for 3 hours. We found all kinds of shells. The fisherman picked us up at 12:30 for $10.00. (Two days wages for him). La Pesca is a neat town with no tourists and warm, friendly people. Don't know the population but about four blocks long, with rough side streets, with pigs all over the town. I don't know how the owners know who owns who. All sizes, from sows to piglets.

Spent the night at the same motel, then up early for the ride home. Took a side trip to La Gotta, a tourist development on the river. Beautiful location on the river bank. Saw a "king fisher" there. It is located near Soto LaMarina.

Back through customs with no trouble. They pulled us over but simply looked into a tool box in back. Got home about 2:00 P.M., after lunch.

Cost for the trip for the three of us was about $35.00 each.

As I have said before, you have fun your way and I will have fun my way.

There is a point to these illustrations. Mexico is an exciting place to tour, no matter how you do it. Yes, I have flown to Mazatlon, Mexico, quickly driven to a very nice resort, but did I really see Mexico? Yet, I did enjoy the pool, the beach, and the waiters who brought my food to the pool. It did cost more than $35.00.

Again, we have visited Cancun, Cozumel, Playa del Carmen, on the East side of Mexico. What is Mexico? Perhaps it can be compared to one who sees the city of New York and concludes that he has seen America.

Visiting Mexico may be like entering a swimming pool, when you are a poor swimmer. It is best to test the shallow water first, then gradually get in over your head. You can start on the border towns, and then go South as far as you, or your budget, will allow you to go.

One QTip stood in amazement when she heard people talking. She quipped, "Even the little children speak Spanish." Welcome to Mexico!

Chapter Seven

Cognitative Reference The RGV
(Or)
The Story of the Rio Grande Valley

A history of the RGV might be a good way to go, but the very word "history" often makes the mind go blank. Maybe, even in teaching religious subjects we can learn to tell stories about subjects. In a survey of both Jewish and Christian schools, the following words came from the students when they were asked to tell all they knew about the Bible:

Adam and Eve were created from an apple tree.
Lot's wife was a pillar of salt during the day, and a ball of fire at night.
Moses led the Hebrews to the Red Sea, where they made unleavened bread, which is bread made without any ingredients.
The first commandment was when Eve told Adam to eat the apple.
The fifth commandment is to humor thy father and thy mother.
The seventh commandment is thou shalt not admit adultery.
According to the Bible, a Christian should have only one wife. This is called monotony.

You know you are heading in the right direction when you leave San Antonio. When you get near Corpus Christi, on Highway 37, you will see a very large sign, " To The Rio Grande Valley." So far so good.

You will eventually find yourself on Highway 77, going south. Be aware that there are some long stretches of land where you will find no gas stations. Do keep your gas tank at an upper reading.

In about two hours you will enter Raymondville, the town most agree is the very top of the Rio Grande Valley. If it is not in the Valley, there are hundreds of Winter Texans staying in the wrong area. The rumor is that QTips love the attitude of the local people in this town. Too, it is just 20 miles West of Port Mansfield, the home of some of the best salt water fishing in the world.

Anything South of this town is in the Rio Grande Valley. If you go far enough to the south you will be in Mexico. Remember, the lower border of the RGV is the Rio Grande River.

The Valley is bordered by the Gulf of Mexico on the East side and the town of Mission appears to be the last town in the Valley as you go to the West.

The Valley is really a "delta" in that the water level is close to the level of the soil surface. From this type of terrain come fruits, vegetables, citrus, to include the red grapefruit for which Texas is famous.

In any event, you have found your way to the Valley, where thousands of Winter Texans live in cold months.

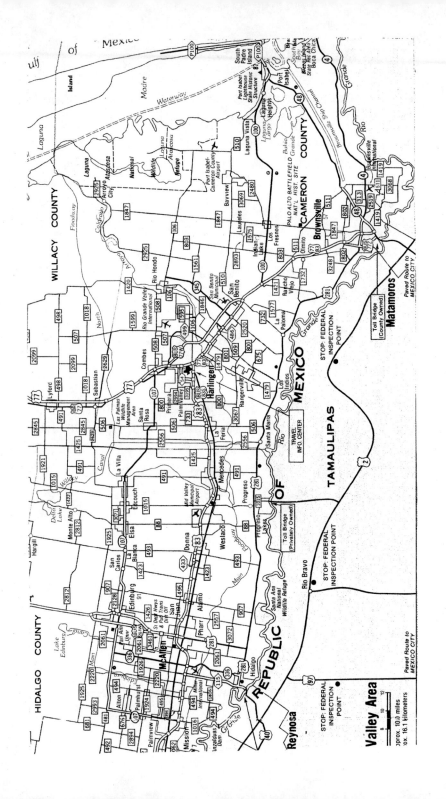

You know you are getting old when.....

The gleam in your eyes is the sun hitting your bifocals.
You feel like the morning after the night before, and you haven't been anywhere.
Your little black book contains only names ending in M.D.
A dripping faucet causes an uncontrollable bladder urge.
You sink your teeth into a steak and they stay there.
You turn out the light for economic rather than romantic reasons.
Your back goes out more than you do.
The gray haired lady you help across the street is your wife.
You just can't stand people who are intolerant.

Will Rogers once said, "People talk about the weather but no one does anything about it." The RGV has some very nice weather, as well as some other types few people like, but can do nothing about.

The latitude of the lower valley is 26.25 degrees North. This is about the same as Ft. Lauderdale, Florida, and the resort of Loreto on Mexico's Baja California peninsula.

Again, in the lower portion the mean temperature is 73 degrees with an average rainfall of 27 to 30 inches each year.

Two locals, trying to get their locked car opened, were using a clothes hanger. "Hurry", said one, "It looks like it will rain and we have to get the top of the convertible up!"

There may be some myths going around that the climate in the Valley is perfect during the winter months. It is called "sub-tropical", whatever that means.

It means that anything can happen! When a storm front carrying a lot of cold air sweeps down from the upper United States, there are no real road blocks at the entrance to the Valley. There are times that the cold weather gets to the Valley. One QTip, always griping about something, commented, "From reading the weather report from where we live, we would be better off back home." Another responded," so would we."

Cold air finds its way to the Valley for short periods of time, then moves across the Gulf and invades Florida. There have been devastating freezes that have wiped out the citrus industry for years and years. It does snow in the Valley, with a few flurries of snow in Brownsville in 1997. Although the flurry was short and light, it was the first time most children had ever seen snow.

As you get closer to the coastal regions you will feel a bit more wind. The average velocity of wind on the Island is 11.4 MPH. It can get cool on the Island, but the same winds make the summers most pleasant.

As for hurricanes, Winter Texans need not worry about them during the times they are normally living in the Valley. Hurricanes are most likely to develop from the month of June, through the month of November.

Hurricanes are a possibility if you return during the warm months. A recent report suggests that ten tropical storms will form between June 1 and November 30. Six hurricanes will form from the tropical storms, and two of the six will be of high intensity, with winds over 111 miles per hour. Statistics show there are an average of nine tropical storms, six hurricanes, and two intense hurricanes, annually. The problem rests in the fact that no one knows just where they will strike.

Among the worst was Hurricane Beulah, which hit the Valley in September, 1967, causing $100 million in property damage and $50 million in crop losses. Flooding caused 13 deaths and 937 injuries. Across Texas the storm spawned 115 tornadoes, the most of any storm in history.

Michael Stephenson writes, "Winnipeg and Fargo are noted for some pretty rugged winter blows. So is Minneapolis, but the worst of all is Buffalo, N.Y. It's because the city of Buffalo is at the precise point where all the cold air from Canada meets all the hot air coming out of Washington."

South Padre Island is reportedly warm because of the warm air coming off the Gulf of Mexico. Another reason is told in a story in the Port Isabel Press, September 26, 1974.

Sigsbee Deep Padre Asset

"One of nature's strangest marine quirks is one of Padre Beach's greatest assets. It is Sigsbee Deep, a tremendous canyon in the floor of the Gulf of Mexico a

few miles from the southern tip of Pa(?)
Sigsbee Deep is approximately 300 mile(?)
miles wide, and it has a uniform depth of (?).
The presence of this large pool of warm water n(?)
beach is generally considered to be at least partially
responsible for the area's warm year-around climate and
beautiful marine life."

In conclusion, (if there is one) the Valley has some very nice weather during the cold months. Just be sure to understand that nothing, anywhere, is perfect.

You Know You Are Getting Old When....

Everything hurts and what doesn't hurt, doesn't work.
You get winded playing chess.
Your children begin to look middle-age.
You finally reach the top of the ladder and it's leaning against the wrong wall.
You're still chasing women, but can't remember why.
You sit in a rocking chair and can't make it go.
Your knees buckle and your belt won't.
You're 17 around the neck, 42 around the waist, and 96 around the golf course.
Dialing long distance wears you out.
You get exercise acting as pallbearer for your friends who exercised.

The Rio Grande Valley has an exciting history. It might be appropriate that we start with the early inhabitants, the Karankawa Indians, in about 1550. Do remember, a story is better remembered than a history.

It would be hard to develop a John Wayne movie in a fight with this bunch of Indians. Though they did use some form of a bow and arrow, they relied heavily on long cane spears. They did not ride horses, and their diet was a bit different. To put it bluntly, they ate people. This was the only cannibal tribe known on this continent.

Some historians claim they ate their enemies only as a part of a ceremonial rite, while others say they made a diet of human beings.

We are talking about an era when the tribes seem to have been the sole occupants of the Valley.

Of course this was before prohibition was lifted on alcohol, so they brewed a drink made from "youpon leaves." It seems this brew might well lay you out very quickly.

The tribe seemed to migrate towards the Island side of the Valley, because they liked to eat fish as well as people. They had it both ways, if the story is true that they lured sailors to the beaches by tying lanterns to many donkeys, making the sailors mistakenly head for a closer voyage with a fleet that turned out to be the churning waters of the beach.

The most well known story is about the 300 Spanish survivors from a shipwreck, who were tracked down and killed as they tried to get to Tampico.

No one really knows what happened to this tribe. It is speculated that they were run off by the early colonists in Austin. Too, rumor has it that LaFitte was asked to get rid of any of them he ran across.

Meanwhile, back at the ranch, Moses and Stephen F. Austin were getting interested in the area that would one day be Texas. A colony was developed as people filtered into the fold, and after some years a provisional government was established at San Felipe on May 3, 1835.

A year later, this new colony decided to claim their independence from Mexico. Santa Anna, from down South, had no sense of humor about the idea of these folks claiming part of what he considered his property. The Valley, as well as much as two-thirds of what we know as Texas, was up for grabs.

The one thing most people remember is the battle at the Alamo. This Texas Revolution displayed the tactics of Santa Anna, namely to use 100 troops for every single troop on the other side. This was no war. It was a massacre!

The bloody end at the Alamo is still the battle cry of Americans. For the next nine years, and even until this day, the haunting memory of the atrocity lingers.

Even after this incident, Santa Anna still controlled a large part of what we now know as Texas. Although there were negotiations as to the various boundaries, even before the battle, the lines were vague, and the Valley was still claimed by Mexico to be their property.

The skirmishes continued for a long time and neither the Mexicans or the Americans really knew who owned the fertile Valley. To bring this dispute to an end, and after Texas became a part of the United States General Zachery Taylor was sent to the Rio Grande area.

The result, the Mexican War, had better odds for us!

General Taylor moved a large force from New Orleans to the mouth of the Rio Grande Valley. The playing field was now level. After establishing Fort Brown, around which Brownsville was developed, the General proceeded to secure the line, The Rio Grande River, as the boundry between Mexico and The United States.

This war was over in two years.

Break Time

If at first you don't succeed, destroy all evidence that you have tried.
A conclusion is the place where you got tired of thinking.
He who hesitates is probably right.
No one is listening until you make a mistake.
Success always occurs in private, and failure in full view.
To succeed in politics, it is often necessary to rise above your principles.
A clear conscience is usually the sign of a bad memory.
Monday is an awful way to spend 1/7th of your life.
If you must pick between two evils, pick the one you've never tried before.
Change is inevitable, except from vending machines.

** The exam at the end of this book only covers the serious material.**

The next war to have direct impact on the Valley was the Civil War. Even as far away as it might appear, a lot of action took place in the Valley, primarily near the coastal areas, to include Brownsville, Port Isabel, and South Padre Island.

The lighthouse in Port Isabel was the focal point of both the Union and Confederate Armies. The latter first occupied the tower, using it as an excellent platform for directing fields of fire and observing the Union Army slipping down from the north.

When it looked like the Confederates were going to loose the lighthouse, the commander gave the order to destroy it. The attempt failed and the old lighthouse now belonged to the North.

In any combat organization there is someone, or some unit, that fails to get the word. Neither side knew that General Robert E. Lee had surrendered to General Ulysses S. Grant.

Three hundred Union troops marched on Fort Brown and met the Confederates on May 12, 1865. This last battle named the "Battle of Palmetto Hill" was fought 33 days after the official end of the Civil War.

In all its glorious history, any military organization has either the lack of communication, as in this case, or someone fails to understand the orders as directed.

General Grant is said to have asked his "dumbest captain" to read every order he issued. His thinking was that if that officer could understand it, anyone could understand the order. If you are ever called a "Grant's captain", be advised that it is not a compliment.

World War I, the war to end all wars, seemingly did not accomplish that lofty goal. Later. another war, World War II, would be the focus of attention, sacrifice, and patriotism of people in America, to include those in the Valley.

The Valley experienced the same as all other sections of the Nation as young men and women went to war. Many did not return.

There was some close action near Padre Island, as a large number of German submarines were spotted in the Gulf of Mexico. One pilot, in a single engine aircraft spotted one south of Corpus Christi, He first thought it was a strange shadow under the water, but then concluded that it was a U-Boat in 150 feet of water. In one attack, with one bomb, the pilot destroyed U-166, a German invader off the coast of the Rio Grande Valley.

There were many training bases in the valley to train troops of many services. Padre Island was used to help pilots gain skill in hitting targets below.

A report was released that indicates that the Island was one of five areas selected on which to test the Atomic bomb. Fortunately, the Island was not the choice of the five options.

The end of the war came with the dropping of the bomb on Hiroshima by LTC (later to become a General) Paul Tibbetts. Bill Murphy, of the Sandia Lab News, March 13, 1998, quotes General Tibbetts as saying, "At the Pentagon, they're still handing out Purple Hearts that were originally ordered to be made for the invasion of Japan."

The Valley, like the rest of the United States, enjoyed a period of peace and prosperity after the end of World War II. Veterans returned to college, men and women began to build new lives, and the feeling of most was that all was well.

On June 25, 1950, the North Korean Army opened fire on troops below the 38th parallel, first with heavy artillery, followed by infantry and heavy armor. The Korean Conflict had begun.

President Harry Truman sent the 7th fleet into the area as a show of force, and then asked the United Nations for help in stopping the aggression.

The tide of that conflict turned with the famous "Inchon Landing", under the command of General Douglas MacArthur. Finally, an agreement was signed.

It was during this time in history that John Tomkins began his quest of developing South Padre Island into a resort area.

Many Valley men and women were called to serve in the next conflict, this time in The Republic of South Vietnam. Many were wounded, many killed, and many returned when a truce was signed.

During the years to come, men and women of the Valley served in the Panama Canal expedition, the Grenada evacuation, the Gulf War, and Bosnia.

In an earlier chapter I suggested that this generation of Americans experienced a great deal of turmoil, changing the way we look at the world, changing the pattern of the family, and changing the values we hold.

The residents of the Rio Grande Valley shared in this era of change.

For All Those Born Before 1940
We Are Survivors! Consider The Changes We have Witnessed.

We were born before television, frozen foods, Xerox, plastic, contact lenses, Frisbees and the PILL. We were before radar, credit cards, split atoms, laser beams and ballpoint pens.

We got married first and then lived together. In our time, closets were for clothes, not for "coming out of." Bunnies were small rabbits and rabbits were not Volkswagons.

We thought fast food was what you ate during Lent. We were before gay rights, computer dating, dual careers, day-care centers, group therapy, FM radios, tape decks, electronic typewriters, artificial hearts, and guys wearing earrings. A chip meant a piece of wood.

Pizzas, McDonalds and instant coffee were unheard of. We hit the scene where there were 5 and 10 cent stores, where you bought things for 5 and 10 cents. For one nickel you could make a phone call, buy a Pepsi or enough stamps to mail one letter and two postcards. We could buy a new Chevy coupe for $600, and gas was 11 cents a gallon.

In our day, GRASS was mowed, COKE was a cold drink and POT was something you cooked in. ROCK MUSIC was a Grandma's lullaby and AIDS were helpers in the principal's office.

We were certainly not before the difference between the sexes was discovered, be we were surely before the sex change. We made do with what we had, and we were the last generation that was so dumb as to think you needed a husband to have a baby.

No wonder we are so confused and there is such a generation gap today! But we survived! What better reason to celebrate?

    The story of the Rio Grande Valley is much like the story of the changing in America. True, we remain interested in the boundaries of the RGV, the type of weather we can expect, and the history of this warm and fertile land. This is what this chapter has been about.
    We have learned that "Experience is something you don't get until just after you need it."

Chapter Eight

Our Portentous Linear Asylum
(Or)
Our Changing Family Structure

No one can say for sure when the American family began its gradual change. Some say it began during World War I, while others place the change in the hard years between World War I and World War II. Almost everyone agrees that the latter war dramatically changed the family structure once held as sacred in America.

When most QTips were born, the family was united in a close relationship with grandparents, parents, children, cousins, uncles and aunts, and brothers and sisters. Although there were dysfunctional families, the normal expectation was that families "stuck together."

Sociologists call this the "nuclear" family. Normally the family units lived within a few miles of each other. The children attended school with their cousins, and the grandparents served as chiefs of the tribe.

The changing family structure changed due to the effects of speed, war, and industry. It would be almost impossible to know when subtle changes began to happen. The truth is that the family unit we once knew and enjoyed, is no longer the larger part of our world.

Let me use my own life as an example of the change in the World War II era.

During the late 1930's my life was made up of a grandfather, grandmother, dad and mother, three sisters and one older brother. We lived in Arkansas City, Kansas. (We did not pronounce it as "Arkansaw") That lingo belonged to some folks in another part of the United States.

Forty miles north of our home, in Augusta, Kansas, I had an uncle, an aunt, and a cousin. During these years there were deaths in some families, and the circle grew smaller, but it stayed in place.

The early 1940's introduced a changed family life.

My cousin moved to Kansas City.

(In those days a long distance)

My brother was sent to Maine.

(Now we are really talking distance)

My oldest sister moved to Birmingham, Alabama.

My dad was sent to the Rio Grande Valley.

My remaining two sisters went away to work.

My mother and I joined dad down south.

My uncle and aunt just stayed put.

In just a few short years, family life, as I once knew it, was over. This was true of most people growing up in that era, who are reading this book today.

Who would venture a guess as to the value of the new world verses the old world? We only know that the family in the United States changed, and that it had impact on all people, including those in the Winter Texan age group, who are trying to find some sense of order in this book. As a result of these changes we have seen the role of older people change dramatically. The role of grandparents is a role up for grabs.

An Ideal Model For Liberated Grandparents?
(Combining the nuclear and extended family role)

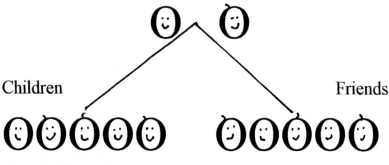

Grandchildren

☻☻☻☻☻☻

Great Grandchildren

☻☻☻☻☻☻☻☻☻☻☻☻

The key is not the number of relationships, but the time spent with each side of the family/non-family units.

The Big Question

What degree of "nuclear" investment of time is OK?
What degree of "non-nuclear" time is OK?
(Sounds like Sociology 101)

This newspaper article was written some 35 years ago and was printed in Omaha, Nebraska. Probably it is my feeble attempt to "lighten up" before we move on.

From Grandparents

When the grandchildren numbered one,
to have you come was such joy, such fun.
When the darlings, the sweethearts, numbered two,
we considered going to see you.
When the number was three, they were dear,
but having you was a problem I fear.
Mercy me, when you came with four,
some one simply had to sleep on the floor.
Now that the grandchildren number five,
when you come we'll manage to survive.
Please, when the number is six or better,
we'll love you all but just write us a letter.

In the next few pages we will break down the various parenting and grand parenting roles of aging people in general, but a specific look at the "models" of QTips. The sequence of models has no bearing on the views or judgement of the author.

Exempt from these studies are Winter Texans who have no children or grandchildren, so this group can go on to more pertinent information about themselves. The models will depict the many roles that parents and grandparents espouse. These models will illustrate the changes in America during the past eight decades. Somewhere in these examples you may find yourself.

Model A

These parents/grandparents live near their youngsters. They take great pride in every accomplishment of the brood. They often get very independent and take a four day vacation to visit a long lost relative. Fortunately, their brood lives within a few miles of the old house they have occupied for years. Maybe this is as close to the nuclear family as we will see in these models.

They are great parents/grandparents but you really know them at an emotional distance. They probably think "Viagra" is a car polish, and for anyone to think they still do "it" is too much to handle. The grand-kids enjoy them for almost ten minutes and then prefer to go play with the neighbor kids. This might be called the "traditional" model.

Model B

These folks are more in the independent mode. They really enjoy their family but also enjoy their extended family of friends. This couple will probably go on two vacations a year, away from their brood, and enjoy, say a cruise, or a vacation in the mountains. They normally come home with gifts for the grandchildren, showing them where they have traveled.

Model C

This model best describes QTips. They enjoy getting away from the cold country, as well as their brood, but miss the brood as soon as they leave. They enjoy their brood, but not the frigid weather that makes bones ache.

Perhaps the most profound conflicts occur when the dad suggests a three month stay, rather than the normal two month stay in the resort. The wife, in most cases, is still attached to the brood. The last month they spend "having fun" turns out to be less than exciting.

It appears that wives are more interested in their brood than their husbands. This might be a judgment call better avoided. Every parent has their own way of showing affection, and feeling closeness to their brood.

The Winter Texan, who wants to claim another identity, enjoys coming to the Valley. Perhaps we need to ask each television station to ask their viewers, **"It is 10:00 P.M. Do you know where your parents are?"**

These people love their children. Repeat after me, "These people love their children." On the other hand, they know they have worked hard all their lives, have been faithful to best rear their brood, and want to kick up their heels.

In all of this discussion we are examining the degree of absence from the brood. For some parents, a four day vacation is enough. For others, a month is more than adequate, while others wish to spend several months on vacation with their peers.

In many cases, parents elect to move away from their brood, perhaps by choice, or by circumstances. The world in which we live is a fast moving world, with fast transportation, economical telephone calling, and of course E-Mail. This points us in the direction of the next model.

Model D

The people who live, without their children, on the Island are like people all over the world. They choose to live in an environment that best meets their needs. The choice is not made quickly or lightly. Most visit the Island to enjoy a short vacation, and end up buying a condo in which to spend longer numbers of weeks. At some point, they decide that this is the type of life they want to have, and make that "very difficult" move.

You will hear the same story of people throughout the Valley. They came for short periods of time and ended up living in the Valley.

In talking to a couple in St. Lucia, I was told they had moved to that Island because they liked it there. I can understand that! The first thing that flashed across my mind was, "What about the family back home?" Even Model D parents have deep concern about their brood.

We can go on a "justification expedition" and explain to ourselves that we get to learn more about our brood when they spend a week, rather than to observe a special day with a child or grandchild. It is true that we learn more about ourselves in those lazy moments of our lives, and we learn about our brood in the same way. I keep my promise that I will not be judgmental about the best model. Like any parent, however, I have this urge to tell the whole world just how I feel about everything. Unfortunately, the world does not really give a rats.

In short, the nuclear family is emotionally intact, no matter how many miles of distance separates it.

"When people become senior citizens they can eat ice cream for breakfast and drink pop anytime of the day they wish."

Model E

About the time we conclude that there are answers to all questions, the game changes. Now we address the "combination family." Like it or not, over one half of the families in America are of this breed. A man with three children from a former marriage, marries a woman with three children from a former marriage.

The choices made in former models remain the same, but the number of people involved increases. When two families are combined into one, the result can be that you have a brood scattered all over the world. You do not think better. You think bigger!

Model F

There is no better way to say it than that one or more of the children dislike one or more of the parents. This can be called the "dysfunctional" family. Hopefully, these conflicts can be resolved, but it takes a lot of work on both sides of the fence.

These models cannot encompass every parent/ child/ grandchild relationship. One tends to find himself in a rather defined model, with varied degrees of involvement.

"A man who says marriage is a 50-50 proposition doesn't understand two things: 1- women, 2- fractions."

There is a "flip side" to this whole situation!

The Scene:

Ma and Pa have lived in the same town for the past forty years. The wooden house may need minor repairs but it has plenty of room for children and grandchildren.

The two have looked forward to the Sunday cookouts that will include all their children and grandchildren, plus great grandchildren.

They have kept the old house, not because they were in need of so much room, but that it was a place for the children to visit. The utility bills are costly, just to keep the house warm, or cool, depending on the season. The lawn is really too much for Pa to handle in his older years. Yet, they hang on, always thinking about the time when the family will be nested around them. They may be terribly disappointed when the realization comes that this is not to be the case.

Of the many children and grandchildren, most moved away to large cities, often far across the United States.

I recently spoke with a couple who had children living in Africa, Fiji, Austin, Hawaii, and another place I fail to remember.

This couple moved to an area where they could at least be close to one of their children.

We are living in an era where some 20 to 30 percent of young families move each and every year. Try as you may, keeping the tribe together is simply not going to be the rule.

Every so often we run across a family that stayed in a specific area. Often, one or more children stay close to the parents. Most often the family is spread out all over the world.

Let's hear it from the QTip generation!

1. We worked hard all of our lives to keep ourselves and our brood warm and full of food.
2. We spent countless hours taking care of our kids and we were always there when they needed us.
3. We do not need to work anymore.
4. The brood is grown.
5. We're out of here!

The Facts of Life

Nobody will ever win the battle of the sexes.
There's too much fraternizing with the enemy.

Friends may come and go,
but enemies accumulate.

Character is what you are.
Reputation is what people think you are.

Times change. Parents try to adjust within their ability. Our children have to go to where the paying jobs are found. Walter Cronkite, of our era, always ended his newscast with, "And that's the way it is."

Chapter Nine

Dissection Parcel Replications
(Or)
Questions And Some Answers

There are many questions that potential Winter Texans, as well as current ones, may have. This is a form used in this chapter to sort them out.

1. <u>What is the proper name for people from the North?</u>
In the early days people from the cold country were called "Snowbirds". Later, to make them feel at home, the term "Winter Texans" was used. In this book the description "QTips" is often used. They all describe the many visitors from the frigid states.

2. <u>How many of these long term visitors come down?</u>
Dr. Vern Vincent, a professor of quantitative methods at UTPA, says some 120,000 live in the Valley during the peak month of February. He adds, "the number of visitors has been growing at about 4 percent annually for the past decade."

3. <u>Are these people all very old?</u>
Not at all. the typical Winter Texan is 68 years old, married, retired, lives in a RV, and stays for over three months.

4. What does the typical wife make for dinner?
Reservations!

5. Why do these folks come to the Valley?
Bill Hethcock of the Valley Morning Star, Oct.13, 1997, writes, "It's a place where it is warm and cheap, and the folks are friendly. They say it's a place where you can hit the beach in November, wear shorts in December and play shuffleboard instead of shoveling snow."

6. How much money does a typical Winter Texan spend while staying in the Valley?
Dr. Vincent says, " The average Winter Texan household spends $1050 per month on expenses while in the Valley."

7. How much money is that when you add it all up?
"As a group", says Dr. Vincent, "Winter Texans contributed $270 million directly to the Valley economy in 1996." Rio Grande Valley Partnership President, Bill Summers, estimates them spending $400 million, and rising.

8. Is it true QTips come to the Valley with a clean shirt and a $20 bill and change neither?
NO. It is just a joke that irritates them.

9. Why do they come to the Valley?
Check number 5, and add "they like it better than Florida or Arizona."

10. Where do people stay and where is the best?
You only get to ask one question at a time.

11. OK, where do people stay in the Valley?
According to the UTPA study, "Seventy-five percent of the Winter Texans live in recreational vehicle motor homes; 8 percent rent an apartment, motel, hotel or condo; 8 percent rent or own a home and 6 percent stay with a friend or relative.

12. Again, where is the best place to live?
Sit in a restaurant and let the Q-Tips tell you the best places. They can get real testy about who got the best deal of the bunch.

13. Where do you find the best prices at a restaurant?
I follow the Winter Texans and come out very well.

14. From where do these Winter Texans come?
Almost 70 percent come from Midwestern states, with about 30 percent of these coming from Minnesota and Iowa.

15. Do these people eat out at restaurants?
You bet! "Spending in Valley restaurants jumps 20 to 30 percent when Winter Texans are visiting", says Filepe Rincones, president-elect of the Valley Chapter of the Texas Restaurant Association.

16. Do Winter Texans help the Valley?
Go back and repeat Chapter 4 to pass the final exam.

17. Will we continue to get more Winter Texans each year?
Someone told me that people over age 65 have 90% of the money in the United States. However, being over 65 I forget who told me that. People are retiring earlier and the baby boomers are getting into the retirement corridor. For the final exam, the answer is YES.

18. Do many QTips decide to stay in the Valley to Live?
We did. A lot of our best friends did, so give it some thought.

19. Are many of the Winter Texans "criminals?"
Probably not. We train our own down here.

20. Will Valley banks let us cash checks from our home banks?
I have heard reports that many banks are most helpful in that arena. They tend to dislike checks that bounce.

21. Do they give hula dancing classes anywhere ?
I have heard they do, but check with your doctor first.

22. Are there strict speed laws in the Valley?
Very much so, but I am told no Winter Texan has driven fast enough to warrant getting a speeding citation. Where we live on the Island, the top speed is 45 MPH, so probably none of us will have problems.

23. <u>Do many Winter Texans elect to buy homes and live permanently in the Valley?</u>
James Herschel, of STN Realty in Harlingen, states, "Every year we see people who decide to stay. They buy homes here- usually smaller homes from $45,000 to $70,000." Since Texas has no State income tax, those who do own property pay a lot of the bills. Again, after talking with many QTip friends, taxes in Texas are well below many states in the colder regions.

24. <u>Where is the water in Mexico safe to drink?</u>
On page 49 in this book I concluded that I did not know the answer. I know that many of my Winter Texan friends do drink the water, and they were fine when I last saw them. Double-check page 49.

25. <u>Are the hospitals in the Valley adequate?</u>
I suggest they are more than adequate and I have been impressed with those medical facilities I have visited.

26. <u>I do not have room in my car for both my spouse and my computer. Any suggestions?</u>
You can always leave your spouse home, and bring the computer. However, in the new Port Isabel library one can have access to a computer. Other libraries provide for the same.

27. <u>Can I get "on line" without paying long distance telephone rates?</u>
Around most larger cities, Brownsville, Harlingen, and McAllen, you can. I can do so from the Island.

28. <u>Just wondering how much it costs to wash clothing for two people in coin operated machines.</u>
Where we live it costs an average of $3.50 to $4.00 a week for the use of the washer and dryer. If you spend far less, you might consider not standing too close to your friends.

29. <u>How has El Niño affected the Valley weather?</u>
The only observation most Winter Texans made in late 1997 and early 1998 was that it was the best season they remembered in several years.

30. <u>How do grocery prices compare to the prices we pay in the North?</u>
They compare favorably. The fruits and vegetables are far more fresh during the QTip season than your friends enjoy back home.

Break Time
A True Story of Winter Texan Adolescent Behavior

Bob went swimming in the Gulf with Wayne, while the wives stayed on the beach. Wayne says, "Since you have a yellow swimsuit, and I have a red one, let's switch and see if our wives notice." "OK", says Bob, "here's my swimsuit." Wayne says, "See you later!"

More Advice For Winter Texans

If at first you don't succeed...well so much for sky diving.

Don't worry about the world ending today...
It's already tomorrow in Australia.
(unless you are in Australia-then start worrying)

Drive carefully.
It's not only cars that can be recalled by their maker.

Outside of a dog, a book is man's best friend.
Inside of a dog, it's too
dark to read.

28. <u>What more can you tell me about the Valley?</u>
I have already told you more than I know!

29. <u>Do RV parks offer varied things for me to do?</u>
One park in the Valley offers 140 organized activities a week. Ask around and you will find that park.

30. <u>Is there good "birding" in the Rio Grande Valley?</u>
Birding is excellent in the Valley. Some say the best in the world. Over 24 million people travel to watch birds. As much as $100 million is spent in the Valley for this type of adventure.

31. <u>Is it expensive to go fishing on commercial boats?</u>
There is a wide array of choices. You can get on a boat and fish in the Laguna Madre for four hours for under $20. On the other hand, when you go out into the Gulf, it will cost about three times that amount in seasons when you can find a good price.

32. <u>Will the description "QTip" be the descriptive name for us from now on?</u>
I do not think so. I have used the term because it is a new and catchy one. As for me, call me a "Snow Bird", "Winter Texan", or "QTip", but do not forget to send me my retirement check each month. Too, some of us do not have enough hair on our head to turn white and qualify us for the newer description.

33 <u>Is there a site on the web I can use to contact others who come down to the Valley?</u>
I am a novice! Believe that I am a novice! However, I am told you can do well on http://winter texans.com, and if it fails to work, remember I told you I was a real novice.

    I certainly do not know all the answers you might ask, and often I fail to know the questions. These 33 questions about wrap it up. I hope I understood the questions.
    Prior to his leaving the Island, a Winter Texan asked me to have dinner with him that evening. He wished to know what kind of food I appreciated, where I wanted to go, and if I was looking for a lot of "ambiance".
    Now mind you, I am from a small town in Kansas, and never learned much about such things. I thought long and hard and came up with an answer. "Sure", I responded, "you buy it and I'll drink it."

Chapter Ten

Godspeed Legions Species
(Or)
Good-bye To Many Friendly People

We have all said, at one time or the other, "Every good thing comes to an end." You have decided you need to get back and take care of things back home. I have come to the conclusion that this book must come to an end as well.

However, before we part, maybe you can help me and at the same time help others who will travel this way. When you get some time, jot down some of your ideas on the forms at the end of this book. If not, again feel free to contact me at ATibbetts@AOL. Com. I am more than happy you bought this book. Maybe I can make enough money writing books to travel to the North.

You have been a real help to the State of Texas. Last year the tourists in Texas left $27.5 billion dollars in our pockets. You helped 464,000 people, directly in the travel industry, remain employed, and they have well earned $9 billion for their efforts.

More than these contributions, you have had a lot of fun and we have had a great deal of fun with you. Who could ask for anything more? We will miss you in church; on the streets; in our complexes; and even at our favorite restaurants.

It's Time To Go Home When..............

Your children and their brood start calling you collect!
Your neighbor gets tired of mowing your lawn.
Uncle Sam wants to see how much you want to
    contribute for the past year.
30,000 "spring breakers" cross the bridge.
Your whole brood wants to visit you at "Happy
    RV Town."

(I went to the doctor last month and wanted to ask,
"Does your mom know you are playing with needles?")

300 square feet of living space feels like 30.
Your brood starts addressing their letters to you with,
    Dear Mr. and Mrs.............
Condo rents double.
Your grandchildren say, "We're sure happy our other
    grandparents stay in our town."
Your daughter calls and asks for Mr. Smith.
Your neighbors back home are tired of playing
    "Neighborhood Watch" all by themselves.
Too much of your nutrition comes from "Sweet &
    Low."
You miss the pet you couldn't stand when you left.
Your car is getting too many rust spots.

   Do drive carefully as you return to your home and brood. Even when you run away from home, they will let you come back.

People in our age group are very special. We were the generation when a handshake was as binding as a long written contract. Our children understand we spent much of our life on foreign soil, fighting wars we did not start, doing without during some long and lean years. (My mother told me I was a depression baby, and she never got over it.)

No matter what you have read in the last 87 pages, most of it was written in jest. You can be proud of what you accomplished in your younger years, and the sense of ethics you had, and continue to employ.

An Island businessman needed to get his money to the local bank. Very hurriedly he placed the brown canvas bag on the roof of his car while he unlocked his car door. He forgot he had placed the bag on the roof and drove off to make his deposit of many checks and over $800.00 in cash.

When he arrived at the bank, he was shocked that his money was not in the seat next to him. It dawned on him that he had left the bag on his car roof. Carefully, he retraced his path back to his business. He could not find the bag of checks and cash.

About one hour later, a mature couple entered his place of business and asked, "Have you lost something today? You look rather dejected!"

"I am dejected", he snapped, "I have lost every dime of yesterday's deposits. How could I be so stupid?"

The Winter Texan couple smiled and asked him if it was in a little brown bag. "Yes", he replied. It even has my name on it."

"We know", answered the couple, "We found it."

We have been called "Snow Birds", "Winter Texans", and "QTips", but we have normally collected the respect of a younger generation who are happy to see an older generation get out of the house and have a good time. I hope I am right!

While Kathy and I were eating at the La Jaiba restaurant on the Island, a lady got up from her table and approached me with the question, "Are you the one who wrote the book on QTips?" I couldn't slide under the table.

It was never my lot in life to be recognized by a stranger so the confrontation did set me back. My first thought was that perhaps I was the oldest one in the restaurant. As it turned out she recognized me from the little picture on the back of the book.

My mind went back to the time Channel 4 newsman, Johnny Goodman interviewed me, but suggested we not give out my address. Now I knew what he meant. About this time I was thinking it might be better if I had eaten at home.

I assured her I did not intend to offend her in my book. She replied, "Do you know what they call us in Arizona?" By this time I was starting to relax because of her passive attitude. Meekly I asked, "What do they call you in Arizona?"

"They tell we winter visitors that we are akin to the Yo Yo. Do you get it?" I admitted I failed to get her point, but was grateful she was so friendly.

"You know, a Yo Yo; back and forth, come and go; back and forth, come and go; back and forth, come and go; back and forth, come and go; back and forth, come and go; back and forth, come and go; back and forth, come and go; back and forth, come and go; back and forth, come and go*

About The Author

Alan Tibbetts spent his early years in Arkansas City, Kansas, as well as along the "barrier reefs" in the Gulf of Mexico.

He graduated from Drake University and Drake Graduate School in Des Moines, Iowa. (Just after General Taylor moved his forces to Brownsville, Texas). See page 31 of this book.

He later moved to Aberdeen, South Dakota, having been told the weather was colder, but because it was a dry cold he would not suffer. He soon learned not to believe everything he was told.

After enduring the frigid days and nights in that nice city he decided to join the Army and perhaps be assigned to sunny, tropical posts. He was ordered to the State of New York, with a subsequent tour to Anchorage, Alaska.

He requested a warm place to serve and the Department of the Army gave him his wish, sending him on his first tour to South Vietnam. Each time he asked for a warm climate, he found himself back in the Mekong Delta.

His wife Kathy, a native of Northwest Missouri, where it can get very cold, finds the Valley, and South Padre Island, a pleasant place to live. Following many years of living in the Valley as Winter Texans, they decided to move permanently to the area, where they currently reside.

Need Another Copy?
($8.95 postpaid)

For a holiday, birthday, special gift?
To explain to your children and grandchildren why you deserted them?
To be nice to your neighbors back home who watch your home?
To explain to your neighbors what you do in the Valley?
To explain to the IRS why you did not get their latest mailing to you?
To get a copy of the one you "loaned" to a friend?

Call
Toll free 1-877-290-5440
Local (956) 761 7307

E-Mail
Atibbetts @ AOL.com

Write
Alan C. Tibbetts
P.O. Box 3183
South Padre Island, Texas
78597